SPIRIT MAN MILLIONAIRES 2.0

The Mirror

John Lewis

Dedication

To my children and grandchildren — my heart and my legacy.

To my brothers, sisters, and my entire family — your love is my anchor.

To the friends who stood with me in the mirror — you kept me steady when the road was long.

This book is for you, and for every seeker who dares to look deeper until they find the truth.

The Kingdom Within.

Table of Contents

Preface

I have been searching for the truth my entire life. Along the way, I discovered something profound: mirrors are everywhere. They are in the still waters of a lake, in the dark screen of a television, in the phone you hold in your hand, in the glass on your wall — each one holding a reflection of who you are in that moment.

For years, I looked into mirrors without fully understanding what I was seeing. It wasn't until I began to see beyond the surface — into the spiritual reflection — that the truth revealed itself. That truth has changed how I live, move, and see the world.

Spirit Man Millionaires 2.0 is not just a title. It is my reality. It is the journey of breaking old shells, embracing my true identity, and living as the Father-Yahweh created me to be — redeemed by Yahshua, and guided daily by the voice and presence of the Ruach HaKodesh.

My prayer is that as you read, you, too, will find the courage to look deeply into your own reflection and step into the fullness of who you are called to be, Spirit Man Millionaires 2.0.

Acknowledgments

*F*irst, all glory to Yahweh the Father; Yehshua, the Son; and Ruach HaKodesh, the Holy Spirit, my constant guide. Every page of this book is born from Your presence, patience and grace.

To my family — children, grandchildren, brothers, sisters — and friends who prayed, encouraged and believed: you are part of this reflection. The delays were not setbacks; they refined the work and sharpened the message.

To every person who shared wisdom, spoke a word in season, or simply believed in me — thank you.

And to you, the reader — thank you for opening these pages and opening your spirit. May you see more in the mirror than you ever imagined, and may you walk in the fullness of Spirit Man Millionaires 2.0.

John Lewis

Prologue

I t started with a dream.

An egg — whole, perfect. Then the shell cracked and life pushed through.

When I woke, I knew: that shell was me. Layers of fear, religion and distraction breaking away to reveal the truth inside. The Spirit said, "Write it now."

This book was born from that moment. It's about the mirrors we miss, the reflections we ignore and the voice of our Creator speaking through them all.

The shell is broken. Let's begin.

Introduction

I Am John Lewis — Spirit Man. Since my baptism at twelve, I've walked with the Spirit of Yahweh, dreamt dreams and seen visions, heard His voice, and felt His Presence near. Those encounters carried me through every valley and lifted me to every mountaintop.

But I kept searching. Not for sermons or noise, but for the truth straight from the Source — the Spirit who created me. That search opened my eyes to something I'd been walking past my whole life: mirrors. Reflections in glass, water, screens, and faces — each carrying messages from the Spirit.

This is my journey. And my challenge to you: look again at the mirrors in your own life until you see the truth staring back.

PART ONE

Chapter 1

THE SHELL BREAKS

---

*I*t came to me in a dream.

A single egg — pure, white, unmarked.

It wasn't rolling, it wasn't sitting in a nest. It was just there, still, as if it was waiting for something.

I couldn't tell at first if it was whole or cracked. My eyes searched for the smallest line, a sign that something was happening inside. And then... I saw it.

The shell was breaking.

There was no sound, but I could feel it.

I could feel the pressure from within — life pushing against the walls that had contained it. And in that moment, I knew: this was me.

For years, I've been carried in the hands of the Creator — being shaped, protected, and prepared. I've been growing in a place where no one could see the changes.

People might have thought I was still, dormant, maybe even forgotten. But inside, there was movement.

Inside, the Spirit was building strength.

The egg is a strange thing. On the outside, it looks fragile. You think one wrong touch and it will break. But on the inside, it is a fortress for what's growing. And when the time comes, that fortress must give way.

Breaking of the shell is not destruction — it's birth.

When I woke up from that dream, I knew the message was clear:

The season of being hidden is over. The shell — the limitations, the fears, the doubts, the waiting — is cracking.

I didn't need to see the whole chick step out. I didn't need to see the wings or the beak. The fact that the shell was breaking was proof enough that life was about to emerge. And not just any life — life with a purpose, life with a calling, life that had been forming in silence but was now ready to speak.

That's why you're holding this book.

Because I believe that just as my shell is breaking, there are others whose shells are breaking too. And when that happens, there's no going back to the safety of being hidden. You step out. You breathe new air. You stretch wings you didn't even know had formed.

This book is the sound of my shell breaking.

The words you're about to read — they've been forming for years. And now they are ready to come into the light.

So here we begin.

...

Reflections

THE SHELL BREAKS

What fears or limitations in your life need to be broken so your true self can emerge?

Chapter 2

THE PHYSICAL MIRROR

*W*hen you wake up in the morning, you don't always want to look in the mirror right away. Not until you're ready. Not until you've prepared yourself to see the reflection staring back at you.

The physical mirror is often the first place we check before facing the world. We all do it—fixing our hair, straightening our clothes, adjusting our posture. Even if you're just walking past a store window, you catch a glimpse of yourself and instinctively shape up.

But let's be honest—sometimes the mirror is the hardest place to look. Not because of our face, but because of what lies behind our eyes. Life brings storms—loss of loved ones, heartbreak, bills piling higher than paychecks, and the weight of debt that feels like chains around the soul. There are two debts that weigh on us: the grief of death, when a mother, a child, or a close friend is gone; and the debt of survival, when bills and responsibilities stack up with no end in sight.

In those moments, we don't see ourselves in the physical mirror. We see sadness. We see weariness. We no longer study our face, our smile, or the light in our eyes. Instead, we check only the basics: Is my shirt tucked in? Does this dress make me look presentable? Does my scarf match? Are my shoes decent enough to get me through the day? The mirror becomes less about me and more about whether the world will notice my brokenness.

The truth is, the physical mirror is all around us—bathroom mirrors, car windows, storefront reflections—but it becomes invisible when we stop truly seeing ourselves. We drift through life half-present, dreaming into a kind of wonderland, distracted by survival. The Word says trouble will come every day. And it's true: some people focus only on the storm. But the Creator is always calling us—calling us to lift our eyes, to step out of the storm, and to walk on water with Him.

The physical mirror, then, is only the beginning. It shows what's on the outside, but if you can't look into the mirror for your physical self, how could you possibly look into the deeper mirror—the one that reflects your soul, your purpose, your becoming?

Reflections

THE PHYSICAL MIRROR

When you look in the mirror, do you see only your appearance, or do you also see the person you are becoming?

Chapter 3

THE UNIVERSAL MIRROR

*T*he Creator designed the universe as His mirror, and when you know how to look into it, you'll see far more than whether your shirt is tucked in or your hair is neat.

When you wake up in the morning and open your spiritual eyes, the first mirror you should check is the one that looks into the heavens. That mirror isn't made of glass — it's made of light, truth, and creation itself. And when you look into it, your Creator will show you exactly who you are. When we understand that — when we know who we are in spirit — everything changes. You start walking differently. You speak with more authority. You carry yourself as if heaven itself is backing you... because it is.

The more you align with that spiritual reflection, the more the world sees it in you. People won't just see you — they'll see the Creator's reflection shining through you. That's when opportunities start to open, when people begin to favor you, when blessings begin to flow in ways you couldn't have planned.

It's not magic.

It's not luck.

It's alignment.

And alignment doesn't just change your reflection, it changes your reality.

Reflections

THE UNIVERSAL MIRROR

How is the world around you reflecting what's inside your heart and mind?

Chapter 4

ONENESS & SPIRIT CONNECTIONS

When I woke up from the dream of the egg, I couldn't shake it. All morning, it stayed with me — that image of the shell breaking, life pushing out. The more I thought about it, the more I began to see connections in my own life.

One of those connections was with my youngest son,

Joey. He had just released a new track called Beverly Hills. I didn't need to hear the whole song — just those first few seconds told me everything. I could hear his spirit in the music. I could feel his hunger to be there — to step into that life, to leave the 9-to-5 behind, to create on his own terms as a producer and artist.

I told him, "That's the reflection you have to stay in."

Your spirit will always show you a vision before your life catches up to it. That vision is your reflection in the universe — the way creation already sees you. When you catch sight of that reflection, you have to lock in on it. You have to keep it in your mind, your heart, and your actions. Because as you hold that reflection, it bounces back into you.

When you remain in that reflection — the one that heaven shows you — it changes everything. People will notice it before you say a word. They'll see it like Moses coming down from the mountain, his face shining because he'd been in the presence of God.

That glow hovers over you.

It pulls people toward you.

It makes them want to pay you more for what you create, to trust you with greater opportunities, to connect you with others they know. It's not just charisma — it's the

Creator's reflection shining through you.

Right now, my son and I are walking in that reflection together. Father and son, both carrying the same light in different ways. And I know that as long as we stay in it — as long as we keep looking into that universal mirror — the right people, the right resources, and the right doors will come to meet us.

Reflections

ONENESS & SPIRIT CONNECTIONS

Where in your life do you feel the strongest connection to the Spirit of Yahweh?

Chapter 5

BECOMING THE REFLECTION

*T*here's a difference between catching a glimpse of your reflection and actually becoming it.

Anyone can have a vision, but the shift happens when that vision becomes your daily reality. That's when the reflection you saw in the Creator's mirror becomes the life you're walking in.

When you become the reflection, it's not about pretending — it's about alignment. Your words, your thoughts, your actions, your posture — they all match the image heaven has of you.

The first time you catch that reflection, it might come in a dream, in worship, or in a deep conversation. But once you've seen it, there's no way it could be unseen. And then you face the choice:

Will you treat it like a passing moment, or will you step into it fully?

Living in that reflection changes how people see you.

You carry an atmosphere. You bring a glow into every space you enter. And that glow is an invitation for others to find their own reflection too.

But make no mistake—this is not an easy thing.

It's not an easy task.

The moment you catch a glimpse of who you are becoming, the attack begins.

The battle starts. The flesh wakes up.

The mind wants to run in ten different directions at once.

That's when you must close your eyes and hold steady.

Keep looking into that mirror the Creator placed in the universe just for you.

And when you've anchored yourself there, return to your physical mirror and remind your mind who you are and who you are becoming.

Reflections

BECOMING THE REFLECTION

What actions can you take today to align your life with the reflection you want to see?

Chapter 6

LIVING SPIRIT MAN MILLIONAIRES 2.0

S pirit Man Millionaires 2.0 is not just a concept—it is my blueprint for living in the reflection. It is the testimony of my life, a life that has been awakened, corrected, and accelerated by the Spirit.

From the time I was a young boy until this very moment, the Spirit has been there. Every visitation, every presence, every comfort, every protection, every teaching—whether I was fully aware of it or not—the Spirit was guiding me. Spirit Man Millionaires 2.0 reminds me of those times, bringing back to my memory that I was never alone. Even when I wasn't conscious of walking in the Spirit, the Spirit was conscious of walking with me.

And when I realized that the best direction for my life was tuning in to the Spirit, everything shifted. Because man has his own spirit, but truth comes when you align your spirit with the Creator's Spirit. When you finally begin to live from your spirit, you can no longer settle for surface answers. You begin to seek truth, and that truth always leads you to Yahweh—the Source of all wisdom, all knowledge, and all understanding.

"This is the realization :"

- Spirit Man — recognizing that life begins in the Spirit.
- Millionaire — living a Kingdom lifestyle without lack, because lack cannot exist where Yahweh's wisdom flows.
- 2.0 — the upgrade, the acceleration, the next level of being.

It begins in the spirit. You speak as if you're already there. You move as if you've already received it. You walk as if the promise has already manifested, because you know it has. You surround yourself with alignment, you move with boldness, you carry multiple streams of blessing into one flow. You expect overflow. You guard the reflection.

This isn't about chasing money. We all had money before, and it did not make us truly rich. True wealth doesn't come from money—it comes from ideas. It comes from dreams. It comes from visions with the instructions Yahweh gives you to bring those visions to life. Money is only a tool __ your servant. Obedience from your dreams and visions are the true currency that bring Kingdom wealth.

Living as Spirit Man Millionaires 2.0 is living as the upgraded version of yourself—the version that knows money will come, but money will never define you. The version that understands wisdom is wealth, purpose is wealth, health is wealth, peace is wealth. When you live in that reflection, you realize you've already been equipped. The testimony of your past proves that Yahweh has always been there, and His Spirit will continue to reveal the way forward.

This is 2.0—living from alignment, living from truth, living from the Creator's image in you. And when you do, every resource, every opportunity, and every connection you need begins to find you.

Reflections

LIVING SPIRIT MAN MILLIONAIRES 2.0

What does living as your highest self — in spirit, soul, and success — look like for you?

Chapter 7

THE SPIRIT IN THE MIRROR

*T*here was a time when I would stand in front of the mirror and only see the outer man. The reflection that stared back at me was measured by the clothes I wore, the expression on my face, or whether I had slept well the night before.

But now it's different. When I look in the mirror today, before I even notice the physical features, I see light. I see the spiritual side of me — the part that can't be dressed in fabric or hidden by shadows. I see the universe in me, the creation of Yahweh alive and breathing.

It's as if my spirit steps forward first, greeting me before my mind can process the physical image. That spirit shines so brightly that by the time my eyes settle on the "outer man," the inner man has already given me the strength to smile, lift my shoulders, and walk out ready for the day.

When you learn to see yourself in this way, every glance in the mirror becomes a confirmation, not a question. You no longer ask, "Do I look good enough?" Instead, you declare, "I carry greatness within me." The mirror is no longer a judge — it is a witness.

This is the moment you begin to decree and declare.

The mirror is no longer just showing you what you look like—it's confirming who you are in the Kingdom. This is where your words take shape. You no longer stand in front of glass just to check your appearance—you stand as one who carries authority.

Declarations are not wishful thinking; they are the voice of Kingdom citizenship. When you say, "I am healed, I am whole, I am provided for, I am more than enough," you are not making empty statements—you are unlocking what heaven already placed within you. The Word says, "The Kingdom of God is within you." That means you are not waiting for a future crown— you carry Kingdom presence now.

And here is the charge: do not move past this chapter until you know your authority. Do not turn the page until you can look in the mirror and feel the Kingdom within you. Because what you decree here on earth is backed by heaven itself. What you loose on earth will be loosed in heaven and what you bind on earth will be bound in heaven.

This is not about sounding spiritual—it's about living as a Kingdom person, right now, right here. Until you know that the words you speak carry the authority of heaven, don't rush forward. Settle it here. Stand in the mirror and decree who you are, and declare what must be.

Reflections

THE SPIRIT IN THE MIRROR

When you look in the mirror , what will you see beyond your reflection?

What is the Spirit showing you about yourself right now?

Chapter 8

THE SPIRIT THAT DRIVES GREATNESS

*T*here's a force that pushes certain people beyond the limits others accept. It's the fire that keeps the runner training at sunrise, the inventor sketching after midnight, the musician practicing a single note until it feels alive. That force is spirit.

When it's present, you can feel it. It doesn't let you settle for "good enough." It whispers in the quiet, urging you to reach higher and push past what you thought possible. It fuels you to work thirty-six hours in the twenty-four the rest of the world is given.

As a boy, a dog once chased me and I scaled a fence nearly seven feet high in one motion. I didn't stop to think. My body responded to the voice of my spirit — the drive to rise above the threat and act without hesitation.

Not every spirit that drives is the right one. Some lead to greatness built on love, mercy, and truth. Others push toward greed or destruction. The difference is your choice. Align with the Spirit that produces love, joy, peace, patience, kindness, goodness, faithfulness, gentleness, and self-control — and your greatness will bless others too.

This is the same Spirit that has been driving me since Yahweh gave me the dream of the egg. From that moment, when I spoke to my son and received confirmation, I have not put down this pen. The Spirit within me has been pouring out everything you are reading here. It educates me, it gives me wisdom, it fuels my boldness, and it guides me step by step.

This is my first official writing, my first published book, and I know without a doubt it is the Spirit that drives greatness within me that is carrying these words. I will not put this pen down until the Spirit says, "Rest."

I am pouring out everything—every truth, every testimony, every revelation—so that this book itself becomes a witness of what the Spirit that drives greatness is capable of.

Reflection

Recall a time when you did something you didn't think was possible. What was driving you in that moment?

Reflections

THE SPIRIT THAT DRIVES GREATNESS

Discover your driving force, and let it align with your God-given purpose.

Chapter 9

LOOK IN THE MIRROR

I encourage you to look in the mirror every single day—not only at the glass on your wall, but at every reflection life places in front of you. The still surface of a lake. A store window. A polished car. Anywhere you catch your image, take a moment and look—not just at your physical image, but beyond it.

At first, you'll only see hair, eyes, and clothes. But if your spirit is awakening, something begins to happen. You stop seeing just you. You start seeing the creation within you. You notice a light, a presence that wasn't visible before.

And here is the key: keep looking. Because your dreams are a certain type of mirror. Your visions are another type of mirror. Look into your imagination and see what was really placed inside you. Some of it is what you desire; some of it is what was given to you. Remember, we were made in Yahweh's imagination.

He said, "Let us make man in our image." That image is still alive in you.

One of the most powerful seasons of my life was when I lived in the Jade building in Brickell, Miami, Florida. I lived on the 27th floor. Every morning I faced the elevator mirror, and every evening when I returned home, there it was again. That mirror reminded me daily of what I had accomplished—of the obedience that carried me through the day.

The elevator opened directly into my private apartment. By the way, this is where the photo on the back of this book was taken—mirrors everywhere. From inside, I saw straight through the glass walls to the ocean. I watched the cruise ships come and go. I saw the horizon stretching endlessly before me. And as I looked out, my spirit began to travel.

My spirit didn't just stay in the apartment—it soared over the water, over the ships, past the horizon, into possibilities my body had not yet reached. My spirit said, "Let's go. Let's go. Let's go." It carried me into the heavens, into memories and revelations. Once my spirit went there, my mind agreed: "I like this." And when my mind accepted it, my body followed. That is the power of the mirror—it doesn't just reflect where you are, it can show you where you're going.

Day after day, I was surrounded by mirrors—elevator mirrors, apartment mirrors, glass reflections everywhere. They were constant reminders that life itself is a mirror. And those reflections carried me beyond the moment into destiny.

The Bible says, "Seek ye first the kingdom of God." Where is the Kingdom? Within you. Stand before the mirror and recognize the Kingdom inside of you. Walk in righteousness, and doors—like that elevator—will open that no man can shut.

The mirrors in life are not here just to show you your face. They are here to remind you of who you truly are.

Look in the Mirror

Look until your reflection becomes your revelation. The Kingdom is within you — live from that truth.

Reflections

LOOK IN THE MIRROR

When your life is full of mirrors, look and look and look __ and be very proud of your reflection.

Chapter 10

YOUR INVITATION

N ow comes the choice: will you step into it and remain there?

Spirit Man comes first—you awaken to your true identity.

Millionaires—living without lack, walking in the abundance of the Kingdom.

2.0—moving at a rapid pace, staying rooted in the reality you've seen in the Spirit.

This is the moment. Every morning, look into the mirror of creation. See the reflection He shows you. Step into it completely. Guard it. Live it. Let it transform your life and the lives you touch.

The shell is already broken. The reflection is already yours. You are no longer becoming—you already are.

Nowadays, everything is a mirror. Whatever you focus on reflects something back to you—the television, your phone, even the people around you. Look at how often we point our phones at ourselves and say, "Let's take a selfie." You capture yourself, yes—but you also capture the whole crowd behind you. That's more than just a photo—it's a living reflection of that moment, of the people who were with you, of the joy you shared.

Think about it. We all carry memories of photos filled with people who loved us, people we loved, and moments that shaped us. When you stand in front of the mirror now, don't just see your outfit. See the Spirit within you that makes you smile, that keeps you at peace no matter what storm rages outside. See the Spirit that gives you strength even when tragedy falls, and allows you to stand strong—not just for yourself, but for others.

Your shell is broken. Your reflection is now. Your time is here. You are Spirit Man Millionaires 2.0.

So look in the mirror again—and start noticing how much more you can truly see in it. Better yet, look into your spiritual mirror and walk in that lifestyle. Because the Spirit is what gives you treasures in Heaven—and those treasures manifest on earth.

Remember our prayer, the one we've repeated countless times:

Our Father who art in Heaven, hallowed be Thy name. Thy Kingdom come, Thy will be done, on earth as it is in Heaven.

That's not just words—it's reality. On earth as it is in Heaven. We are not just waiting for treasures stored up in Heaven; we are living in those treasures now. The Spirit moves us into alignment so that abundance flows now. The millionaire status is now.

And understand this: I'm not preaching money. Money alone does not make you a millionaire. True wealth is everything else—the Spirit, the wisdom, the vision, the peace, the alignment. Money is only a tool, a servant that follows those who stay rooted in Spirit.

This is Spirit Man Millionaires 2.0. It's your time. Keep checking the mirrors around you—they are always reminding you who you truly are

Spirit Man … Millionaires … 2.0 — it's your time. Keep checking the mirror.

Reflections

YOUR INVITATION

Now step into each day to walk closer with the Creator and your true Spirit Man Millionaires 2.0 Self.

About the Author

John Lewis is a man whose life journey is defined by faith, resilience, and vision. From his early days in Trinidad to fifty years of life in the United States, Spirit Man has walked through seasons of hidden growth, breakthroughs, and divine alignment.

Known by many names over the years — "Jerry" to some, "ItchiBaba" to many, and "J Alex Live" on social media — he now walks boldly as Spirit Man. One day, while in his home, he heard a voice call him "Lazarus." He laughed at first, but quickly realized it was a call to his spirit. The story of Lazarus tells of a man who had been in the grave for four days until the Son of God called him forth. For Spirit Man, that moment became a realization — a reminder that after years of seeking truth, his spirit had been called to rise and live fully in its purpose.

Throughout his lifetime, Spirit Man has worn many hats — entrepreneur, promoter, and visionary. He has owned and operated businesses across multiple industries, including limousine and trucking services, a boutique, a coin laundry, and a restaurant-nightclub. His work also extended to environmental services and recycling initiatives for his home country, securing government contracts to build houses, and even running a radio station. Each venture became another chapter in his testimony of perseverance, creativity, and service to both his community and his calling.

Beyond the titles and enterprises, Spirit Man's mission is rooted in leading others to discover their true identity in the Creator's reflection. Through Spirit Man Millionaire 2.0: The Mirror, he invites readers to look beyond the surface, to see the spiritual reflection that reveals their highest calling. His writing blends personal testimony, practical wisdom, and deep spiritual insight that challenges and inspires.

When he's not writing or building his vision, Spirit Man devotes himself to prayer, family, and uplifting others. His life's motto echoes in every page: "Knowing yourself by looking deeply in life mirrors will lead you to the true God within."

Also by John Lewis

A Word from the Author John Lewis, known as Spirit Man, is a teacher, motivator, and author whose mission is to awaken the spirit within. He is the Founder of God Is Ministries (since 2004), where he served the community in Tampa, Florida through a radio program, prayer, and outreach, while also supporting churches in both the United States and the Caribbean. Through his testimony and life journey, Spirit Man reveals the power of knowing oneself in spirit, body, and soul — where wisdom, wealth, and health are discovered.

Prayer

Father Yahweh God, I come to You in the name of Your Son, Yahshua — Jesus Christ — praying in the Ruach HaKodesh, the Holy Spirit. Lord, You know I grew up calling on You as God, Jesus Christ, and the Holy Spirit, and I thank You for giving me wisdom and understanding to also pray with the foundation names — Yahweh, Yahshua, and the Ruach HaKodesh — just as the elders did in the beginning and will in the end. I thank You that You hear my heart in both. May this book touch and transform every reader, releasing life, healing, and revelation, and may every person discover the God within. Amen.

With Gratitude

If this book has touched your spirit, we would love to hear from you. Please email us with your testimony, reflections, or comments at:

✉@ john@spiritmanmillionaires.com

Our journey continues. The second book in this trilogy, SPIRIT MAN MILLIONAIRES 2.1 (The Recovery), will be available October 2025.

The final book, SPIRIT MAN MILLIONAIRES 2.2 (The Rewards), will be released before the end of this year — and will include testimonies not only from my journey but also from readers and partners like you.

If you feel led to help us carry this mission further, you may also reach out by email to explore how you can partner with us.

Together, we reflect, recover, and rise into the fullness of Abba Yahweh's purpose.

With gratitude,

John Lewis

SPIRIT MAN MILLIONAIRES 2.0

"The Mirror "

HalleluYah, Ruach HaKadash

Declaration & Decree from The Mirror

I decree that every time I look into the mirror of my life, I will see the reflection of Yahweh's image within me.

I declare that I was created with purpose, designed in His likeness, and appointed to walk in wisdom, health, wealth, and divine favor.

I decree that my reflections bring revelation—showing me who I truly am in Spirit, body, and soul.

I declare that this day is the day Yahweh has made, and I will rejoice and be glad in it, for I lack nothing.

As I reflect, I recover. As I recover, I am rewarded.

In the name of Yahshua, so let it be.

www.ingramcontent.com/pod-product-compliance
Lightning Source LLC
Chambersburg PA
CBHW031258120626
46545CB00007B/2876